Entrepreneur's Loop

Insights from Serial Entrepreneurs on Starting, Scaling, Exiting, and Repeating

I0446466

Naomi Jaurez

Table of content

INTRODUCTION

START

SCALE

EXIT

REPEAT

NAVIGATING   THE
ENTREPRENEUR'S   LOOP   IN
TODAY'S WORLD

CONCLUSION

- # Defining The Entrepreneur's Loop

In the realm of entrepreneurship, there is a specific rhythm that develops, a pattern that becomes the pulse of this continuous journey. It's the Entrepreneur's Loop, a notion that embodies the eternal cycle of entrepreneurship, distinguished by its four main phases: Start, Scale, Exit, and Repeat.

**The Essence of the Entrepreneur's Loop

The Entrepreneur's Loop is, at its heart, a continual cycle of creativity, creation, development, and rejuvenation. It symbolizes the spirit of entrepreneurship, where each phase is not only a goal but a stepping stone to the next.

- **Start**: This is where it all starts. The birth of a new enterprise, the germination of an idea, and the courageous plunge into the unknown. The Start phase is distinguished by excitement, vision, and the confidence to take that initial move.

- **Scale**: As your enterprise acquires speed, the Scale phase comes into play. This is where you watch the development, expansion, and transformation of your original concept into an actual, impacting reality. It's about creating a firm foundation and pushing the limits.

- **Exit**: The Exit phase is an important milestone in the entrepreneurial path. It entails shifting from one enterprise to the next, whether it is by selling your firm, combining it with another, or taking it public. It's about appreciating the value you've generated and moving on to new challenges.

- **Repeat**: The last step of the loop, Repeat, is about adopting the lessons from prior efforts and beginning on a new cycle of invention. It's a monument to the durability of the entrepreneurial spirit, and the determination to learn, adapt, and start afresh.

- ## The Importance of Serial Entrepreneurship

Serial entrepreneurship is not only a word but a dynamic force that profoundly impacts the business world. It is an idea spoken with awe and wonder, a phrase that signifies a transformational and inventive approach to business. In this part, we look into the importance of being a serial entrepreneur, investigating the influence it has on people, industries, and the greater entrepreneurial environment.

The Catalyst for Innovation

Serial entrepreneurs are accelerators of innovation. They are the innovative brains who continuously question the current quo and seek fresh solutions to chronic challenges. Through their initiatives, they bring new goods, services, and business methods, moving industries ahead. Their capacity to explore, adapt, and repeat gives new insights to the marketplace.

Driving Economic Growth

The value of serial entrepreneurship extends to economic development. These entrepreneurs generate employment, promote local and global economies, and cultivate a culture of entrepreneurship. Their companies typically function as incubators for rising talent, and they give mentoring and chances to other aspiring entrepreneurs, supporting a thriving entrepreneurial environment.

Learning from Experience

Serial entrepreneurs gather essential expertise with each business. They learn from wins and disappointments, building a unique skill set that combines resilience, flexibility, and the capacity to make

4

educated judgments under ambiguity. This information is transportable and helps them to make better-measured risks and informed decisions in succeeding enterprises.

A Legacy of Impact

Serial entrepreneurs often leave a legacy of effect. Their enterprises may reshape sectors, impact social change, and encourage others to start on entrepreneurial paths. Whether via revolutionary technology, sustainable practices, or disruptive business models, they contribute to the benefit of the planet.

A Testament to Resilience

Serial entrepreneurship is a monument to resilience. The capacity to constantly start, scale, depart, and repeat demands a strong resilience in the face of hardship. It entails addressing obstacles head-on, learning from failures, and continuously chasing new chances.

Setting an Example

Serial entrepreneurs set an example for the future generation. Their tales of continual innovation and success serve as beacons of encouragement for young entrepreneurs. They highlight that entrepreneurship is not tied to a single effort but rather a lifetime path packed with intriguing opportunities.

- ## Overview of the Book's Structure

As you begin on your voyage into the realm of the Entrepreneur's Loop and the relevance of serial entrepreneurship, it's crucial to grasp the roadmap that will guide your investigation. This book is meticulously constructed to offer you a complete overview of the subject matter, insights from experienced entrepreneurs, and practical skills to manage your entrepreneurial path.

Start

The trip starts with "Start." In this chapter, we will study the origin of a new endeavor, from envisioning a business idea to taking that adventurous leap into the entrepreneurial world. You'll learn how to improve your ideas, uncover the necessary tools, and handle the early hurdles that come with launching a new enterprise.

Scale

The second chapter takes you into the core of entrepreneurship: "Scale." Here, you will find ways for continued success and progress. Building a good team, growing your market reach, and managing money throughout moments of growth are just a few of the main issues we'll dig into. Scaling your company is an exciting but challenging time, and we're here to assist you in managing it.

Exit

"Exit" is a crucial milestone in the Entrepreneur's Loop. This chapter focuses on knowing when and how to leave a business, whether it's by selling your firm, combining it with another organization, or taking it public. We'll examine the intricacies of shifting from one enterprise to the next and address the emotional implications of parting with a project you've put your heart and soul into.

Repeat

The voyage doesn't finish with an exit; it continues to the "Repeat" phase. Serial entrepreneurs thrive on learning from earlier enterprises and beginning new cycles of invention. In this chapter, we'll look into the serial entrepreneur's attitude, the skill of applying expertise in new ventures, and balancing risk and opportunity as you push into unfamiliar territory.

Navigating the Entrepreneur's Loop in Today's World

The entrepreneurial environment is always developing. In this chapter, we investigate how the

Entrepreneur's Loop adapts to the current business environment. We'll address the importance of technology, innovation, and global views in serial entrepreneurship.
Conclusion
As we conclude our trip, the last chapter serves as a synopsis of the Entrepreneur's Loop. We'll reflect on the continual growth of entrepreneurs and their endeavors and provide support to those who wish to pursue this route.

• The Genesis of Entrepreneurship

In the great expanse of entrepreneurial landscapes, every initiative has a modest beginning, a point of genesis known as "The Genesis of Entrepreneurship." This chapter discusses the birth of a new enterprise, from the spark of an idea to the daring step of initiation. We will dig into the fundamental factors that characterize this phase and set the foundation for the entrepreneurial journey ahead.
Conceiving the Idea
The birth of entrepreneurship generally starts with an idea, a vision, or a concept that fires the entrepreneurial spirit. This section looks into the skill of creating a company concept. You will learn

how to detect possibilities in the market, uncover unmet requirements, and establish a vision that will drive your entrepreneurial pursuits.

From Idea to Plan

A concept alone is not enough. This part discusses the transition of your idea into a feasible business strategy. You'll learn how to design your company model, develop goals and objectives, and construct a plan for your firm. We'll cover the necessity of market research, knowing your target audience, and building a plan that can stand the test of the entrepreneurial journey.

The Audacious Leap

Entrepreneurship is an adventurous adventure, and taking that initial step is frequently one of the toughest components. We'll analyze the guts and drive necessary to establish your enterprise. You'll learn about the hazards, both human and financial, connected with business and how to handle them with confidence.

The Early Challenges

The Genesis period is distinguished by early hurdles, from getting the first money to developing a fundamental staff. This section gives insights for acquiring resources, finding mentors, and navigating the challenges that come with the commencement of a new enterprise. We'll explore typical hurdles and how to overcome them.

The Importance of Adaptability

The origin of entrepreneurship is not a static phase; it's a dynamic and ever-evolving process. You'll get a knowledge of the necessity for adaptation, flexibility, and a readiness to pivot when circumstances change. This flexibility is a feature of successful entrepreneurs who flourish amid the ups and downs of this era.

- ## Identifying and Refining Your Business Idea

The birth of entrepreneurship frequently starts with a spark—an idea that captivates your imagination and fuels the drive to create something new. This chapter is devoted to the skill of discovering and developing your company concept. It's a key milestone in the entrepreneurial path, one that may ultimately influence the destiny of your business.

Recognizing Opportunities

Entrepreneurship is, at its foundation, about spotting

opportunities. This section looks into the process of finding unmet requirements, holes in the market, or difficulties that may be solved via your enterprise. You'll learn how to perform market research, assess trends, and seek out possible possibilities that connect with your interests and talents.

The Power of Passion

Passion is the motivating element behind many great endeavors. This section addresses the necessity of finding a company concept that connects with your interests and beliefs. We'll address how your interests may pour energy and tenacity into your entrepreneurial career, making the long and tough route more rewarding.

Refining Your Vision

Having an idea is one thing; developing it into a viable company plan is another. This section helps you through the process of developing your vision, establishing your value proposition, and identifying your unique selling characteristics. You'll learn how to turn your concept into a captivating story that connects with your target audience.

Evaluating Feasibility

Entrepreneurial success relies on more than simply a fantastic concept; it rests on practicality.

This section digs into examining the viability of your company concept. You'll learn how to perform feasibility studies, analyze risks, and identify possible bottlenecks. Understanding the viability of your concept is a vital step in building a sustainable enterprise.

Seeking Feedback and Validation

No concept is perfect from the start. This section stresses the necessity of getting input and validation for your company plan. You'll study ways to get advice from prospective consumers, mentors, and industry experts. Feedback might lead to essential revisions and boost your idea's market fit.

The Iterative Process

Refinement is an iterative process. Entrepreneurs typically find themselves reviewing and changing their ideas as they acquire new insights and criticism. We'll cover the dynamic nature of developing your company idea and how adaptability is a crucial aspect of entrepreneurial success.

- ## Navigating the Early Challenges

The early phases of entrepreneurship may be a proving

ground for your commitment, ingenuity, and flexibility. This chapter is devoted to understanding and negotiating the early hurdles that every entrepreneur confronts as they commence on their path to developing an idea into a sustainable company.

Defining Early Challenges

Early hurdles in entrepreneurship are varied and dynamic. This section gives an overview of typical challenges, such as limited resources, market uncertainty, and competition. It lays the scene for a deeper study of how to overcome these difficulties.

Resource Constraints

Financial limits, a lack of equipment, and restricted access to experienced personnel are frequent problems encountered in the early phases of an enterprise. This section covers ways for managing and making the most of restricted resources. It explores cost-effective solutions, lean approaches, and innovative problem-solving.

Market Validation and Customer Acquisition

Gaining momentum in the industry and obtaining the first consumers may be daunting jobs. This section covers the necessity of market validation and how to test your ideas with actual clients. You'll learn how to identify your target customer, establish a value proposition that resonates, and successfully sell your goods.

Competition and Differentiation

Competition is an intrinsic component of entrepreneurship. This section digs into techniques for distinguishing your enterprise from rivals, whether via innovation, greater customer service, or distinctive positioning. It underlines the necessity of analyzing your competitive environment.

Pivoting and Adaptation

The capacity to pivot and adapt is a characteristic of successful businesses. This section covers when and how to pivot your company plan depending on market input and developing conditions. You'll discover how to preserve flexibility while keeping committed to your primary vision.

Mentorship and Guidance

Seeking assistance and mentoring is a good method for overcoming early hurdles. This section explains ways to discover mentors, advisers, and industry professionals who may give insights and help. Mentorship may bring the insight and expertise to traverse rough seas.

Emotional Resilience

Entrepreneurship typically entails emotional ups and downs. This section highlights the significance of emotional resilience, handling stress, and having a positive outlook. You'll find ways to deal with the issues that might often seem overwhelming.

- ## Funding and Resources for the Launch

Launching an entrepreneurial enterprise takes more than just a wonderful concept; it necessitates the resources and money to convert that idea into a reality. This chapter is devoted to understanding the financial elements of entrepreneurship, from acquiring finance to identifying critical resources for a successful launch.

Understanding Your Financial Needs

Every business journey starts with a clear grasp of financial requirements. This section discusses how to determine your starting costs, running expenditures, and financial predictions. It's a key step in acquiring the required resources for a flawless launch.

Bootstrapping and Self-Funding

Many entrepreneurs start their enterprises with their finances, a strategy known as bootstrapping. This section examines the pros and difficulties of self-funding and gives insights on how to make the most of your resources while beginning your firm.

Seeking External Funding

For businesses with more extensive financial demands, external investment may be needed. This section goes into several financing possibilities, including angel investors, venture capital, crowdsourcing, loans, and grants. You'll learn how to construct a great proposal and attract possible investors or lenders.

The Importance of a Strong Business Plan

A comprehensive business plan is a key document in your hunt for finance. This section leads you through the preparation of a thorough business plan that contains your vision, tactics, and financial estimates. You'll learn how a well-structured strategy may build trust in prospective investors and lenders.

Leveraging Networks and Relationships

Networking is a crucial resource for prospective businesses. This section addresses the value of creating connections with mentors, industry colleagues, and possible investors. It demonstrates how these relationships may open doors to financing possibilities and extra resources.

Identifying Essential Resources

Beyond finance, beginning a startup needs access to crucial resources, from technology and infrastructure to people and coaching. This section presents a checklist of resources that may help you develop a good foundation for your firm.

Government Programs and Incentives

Government initiatives and incentives may give vital help to entrepreneurs. This section exposes you to numerous government programs, grants, and tax benefits that help lessen the financial strain of beginning a company.

Mitigating Financial Risks

Entrepreneurship is not without hazards, and learning how to reduce these risks is crucial. This section outlines ways to control financial risks and build a safety net for your enterprise.

• Growth Strategies for Sustained Success

The Scale phase in the Entrepreneur's Loop indicates a crucial turning point, as your venture changes from its earliest stages to a time of development and growth. This chapter is devoted to analyzing growth techniques that will pave the road to sustainable success in your entrepreneurial journey.

Defining Growth in Entrepreneurship

Growth is a multidimensional term in entrepreneurship. This section gives an overview of what growth means in the context of your endeavor, whether it entails raising revenue, extending market reach, or attaining other business objectives.

Customer-Centric Growth

Growth begins with knowing your clients. This section examines the necessity of having a thorough knowledge of your target customer, listening to their requirements, and adapting your goods or services to fulfill those needs efficiently.

Scaling Operations

As your venture expands, your operational demands get more complicated. This section addresses how to expand your operations effectively, manage resources, and build systems that can meet the additional needs of a growing organization.

Strategies for Market Expansion

Expanding into new markets may be a vital growth strategy. This section discusses how to find and penetrate new markets, whether they be geographic, demographic, or specialty markets. It addresses the necessity of market research and localization.

Product and Service Diversification

Diversifying your product or service offerings may be a crucial driver of development. This section goes into tactics for introducing supplementary goods or services, cross-selling to current clients, and increasing your business's value offer.

Building a Strong Team

A competent and motivated staff is vital for continued success. This section highlights the necessity of hiring, keeping, and creating a high-performing team. It also offers ways to establish a good and creative company culture.

Financial Management for Growth

Managing funds throughout expansion is a vital component of

success. This section covers ways for financing expansion, whether via reinvested earnings, external capital, or debt. It addresses financial planning, budgeting, and financial risk management.

Marketing and Branding for Growth

Effective marketing and branding are vital to express your value offer to a bigger audience. This section digs into growth-oriented marketing methods, including digital marketing, content marketing, and branding approaches that build awareness and trust.

- ## Building a Strong Team

One of the most crucial components in the success of any enterprise is the people behind it. This chapter is devoted to understanding the art of developing a strong and effective team, a cornerstone of entrepreneurship and a crucial driver of success throughout the Scale phase of the Entrepreneur's Loop.

The Team's Role in Your Venture

Before getting into the tactics for developing a great team, it's crucial to grasp the pivotal function that your team plays in your endeavor.

This section gives an overview of how your team affects your company's culture, performance, and capacity to reach your development objectives.

Defining Your Team's Needs

The first step in developing a good team is to determine your team's requirements. This section outlines how to determine the main jobs and skill sets necessary to support your business's development. It also underlines the significance of developing a team that complements your skills and fills in the gaps.

Recruitment and Hiring Strategies

This section discusses tactics for recruiting and hiring, including writing engaging job descriptions, accessing the proper talent pools, and performing successful interviews. It also gives insights on how to analyze applicants for cultural fit and their alignment with your company's values.

Retaining Top Talent

Recruiting excellent talent is merely the beginning; keeping them is vital. This section goes into tactics for keeping your finest team members, including giving competitive salaries, providing growth and development opportunities, and establishing a work atmosphere that supports job satisfaction.

Effective Onboarding

Once you've created your staff, onboarding is a key step. This section describes how to design an efficient onboarding process that helps new team members integrate quickly into your company's culture and processes. It underlines the necessity of having clear expectations from day one.

Fostering Collaboration and Communication

Collaboration and efficient communication are crucial to a great team. This section discusses techniques for fostering an open and collaborative work atmosphere, from frequent team meetings to employing technology for seamless communication.

Building a Diverse and Inclusive Team

Diversity and inclusion are not just ethical imperatives but also drivers of innovation and success. This section highlights the advantages of establishing a diverse team and tactics for promoting an inclusive workplace culture.

- # Expanding Market Reach and Customer Base

Market growth and extending your client base are crucial to establishing continuous success throughout the Scale phase of the Entrepreneur's Loop. This chapter is devoted to analyzing ideas and techniques for increasing your reach, gaining new clients, and establishing your place in the market.

Defining Market Expansion

Before getting into the tactics, it's crucial to clarify what market growth means for your business. This section gives an overview of the many strategies to increase your market reach, whether via regional growth, demographic targeting, or entering new niches.

Market Research and Segmentation

Successful market growth starts with in-depth market research and segmentation. This section highlights the necessity of identifying your new target markets, researching consumer habits, and segmenting your audience to adjust your strategy efficiently.

Multi-Channel Marketing
Reaching new markets typically includes multi-channel marketing activities. This section discusses tactics for reaching your target audience via numerous channels, including digital marketing, conventional advertising, social media, content marketing, and email marketing.
Localization and Cultural Considerations
Expanding into new markets, particularly worldwide, demands cultural awareness and customization. This section goes into how to adjust your goods, message, and tactics to meet the cultural subtleties of your target markets.
Partnerships and Alliances
Collaborating with other firms and developing strategic alliances may be a significant approach to market development. This section explains how to locate suitable partners and develop mutually beneficial connections to access new clients.
Scaling Customer Acquisition
Customer acquisition is crucial to market growth. This section discusses ways to grow client acquisition, from improving your website and landing pages to employing paid advertising and using user-generated content.

Retention and Customer Loyalty

While recruiting new consumers is critical, keeping and growing client loyalty is crucial. This section goes into ways to offer exceptional customer service, build loyalty programs, and foster long-term connections with your consumers.

Evaluating Market Expansion Success

Measuring the performance of your market growth activities is crucial. This section describes how to define key performance indicators (KPIs), monitor your progress, and adapt your tactics depending on the outcomes you obtain.

- ## Managing Finances Amid Growth

Managing your money throughout the expansion period of your firm is a vital component of obtaining continuous success in entrepreneurship. This chapter is devoted to discussing ways to properly control your money as your firm develops and encounters new financial issues.

Financial Planning for Growth

Before getting into the techniques, it's vital to create a good basis for financial planning. This section highlights the necessity of constructing a financial development plan, defining clear financial targets, and developing a budget that matches your growth goals.

Cash Flow Management

Cash flow is the lifeblood of every organization, and its management becomes even more crucial during expansion. This section discusses ways to properly manage your cash flow, maximize your working capital, and ensure you have the financial means to support your growth.

Investment and Capital Allocation

As your firm expands, you may need to invest funds for numerous goals, including recruiting, technology, infrastructure, and marketing. This section outlines ways to manage your cash properly to assist your growth ambitions.

Financial Risk Management

With expansion comes new financial dangers. This section discusses ways for recognizing and managing financial risks that may develop throughout the growth, from market risks to operational and financial risks.

Financing Options

When company development demands more funding, knowing your financing choices is vital. This section addresses several forms of finance, including equity investment, debt financing, and other funding techniques, and how to pick the most suited choice for your firm.

Profitability and Growth

Profitability is the ultimate measure of success. This section digs into tactics for preserving and enhancing profitability while managing your business's development, including pricing strategies, cost management, and revenue improvement.

Measuring Financial Performance

Measuring financial performance is a constant activity. This section highlights the major financial metrics and key performance indicators (KPIs) that you should measure to analyze the financial health and success of your developing firm.

Financial Reporting and Transparency

Transparency and good financial reporting are vital for stakeholders, investors, and internal decision-making. This section covers how to build transparent financial reporting processes and convey financial information effectively.

• Knowing When to Exit

The Exit phase in the Entrepreneur's Loop highlights a key crossroads in your entrepreneurial path. Knowing when to abandon an enterprise is a choice that demands serious study and strategic strategy. This chapter is devoted to addressing the key components of recognizing when and how to depart your company effectively.

The Significance of the Exit Phase

Before getting into exit plans, it's crucial to grasp the importance of this phase in the entrepreneurial journey. This section gives an overview of the numerous circumstances and incentives that might lead to an exit, whether by selling your firm, merging with another company, or taking it public.

Defining Exit Goals and Objectives

Exit plans are not one-size-fits-all; they should coincide with your aims and objectives. This section addresses how to identify your exit objectives, whether they entail optimizing financial gains, shifting to a new enterprise, or seeking a lifestyle change.

Exit Planning and Timing

Strategic exit preparation is a vital part of a successful exit. This part discusses the significance of timing, preparing your firm for sale, and building an exit strategy that optimizes value while avoiding risks.

Selling Your Business

Selling a firm is one of the most typical departure methods. This section goes into the process of selling your company, from appraisal to locating possible buyers, negotiating terms, and closing the transaction. You'll also learn about due diligence, a critical element of selling a firm.

Mergers and Acquisitions

Merging with another firm or being purchased might be a lucrative exit plan. This section explains how to find prospective merger or acquisition prospects, negotiate terms, and manage the transfer efficiently.

Going Public (IPO)

Taking your firm public via an Initial Public Offering (IPO) is a key exit option. This section discusses the process of going public, from preparing your firm for the IPO to negotiating the regulatory and compliance requirements.

Alternative Exit Strategies

Not all exits fit the standard molds. This section addresses alternate departure methods, such as leaving your firm to a family member, organizing a management buyout, or pursuing a phased exit over time.

Legal and Financial Considerations

Exiting a company entails legal and financial complexity. This section gives insights into the legal and financial elements of departing your firm, including tax issues, legal contracts, and the significance of competent consultants.

Life After Exit

The entrepreneurial journey doesn't stop with the exit; it leads to new opportunities. This section discusses the chances and problems that arise after departing an enterprise, whether it entails retirement, new initiatives, or other efforts.

- ## Various Exit Strategies (e.g., Selling, Merging, IPO)

Exit plans are crucial in the entrepreneurial process and should fit with your objectives and the stage of your firm. This chapter discusses several exit plans, from selling your firm to combining with another company and going public via an Initial Public Offering (IPO). Understanding these possibilities is vital for making educated decisions regarding the future of your organization.

Selling Your Business

Selling your firm is one of the most popular and easy exit plans. This section looks into the process of selling your company, including the important phases of appraisal, preparing your firm for sale, seeking possible buyers, and negotiating terms. It also handles due diligence, a rigorous assessment of your business's assets, obligations, and possible dangers by prospective purchasers.

Mergers and Acquisitions (M&A)

Merging with another firm or being purchased might bring options for development and exit. This section discusses how to discover possible M&A prospects, negotiate terms, and manage the integration process efficiently. You'll learn about the many kinds of M&A agreements, such as horizontal, vertical, and conglomerate mergers, and how to identify the most suited one for your scenario.

Initial Public Offering (IPO)

Taking your firm public via an IPO is a crucial exit option that gives the ability to acquire cash and obtain liquidity for shareholders. This section goes into the complexity of going public, including preparing your firm for the IPO, managing regulatory and compliance requirements, and the process of issuing shares to the public. You'll also learn about the pros and pitfalls of going public and considerations surrounding the timing of your IPO.

Alternative Exit Strategies

Not all exits fit traditional molds. This section outlines alternate escape methods that you might explore, based on your circumstances. Options include transferring your firm to a family member, executing a management buyout, or pursuing a phased retirement over time. Each of these potential tactics has specific benefits and problems that you should carefully examine.

• Preparing Your Business for a Smooth Transition

Exiting a firm is a key stage in the entrepreneurial path, and the success of your transition primarily rests on meticulous planning. This chapter is devoted to discussing ideas for preparing your company for a seamless and successful transition, whether via a sale, merger, IPO, or other exit plan.

The Importance of Preparation

Before getting into the tactics, it's vital to underline the value of preparation in the leaving process. This section covers the primary reasons why planning is vital for a seamless transition and the advantages it delivers to both you and possible purchasers, partners, or investors.

Financial Transparency and Documentation

Financial openness is crucial during a transformation. This section highlights the need to keep accurate and transparent financial records, including balance sheets, income statements, tax filings, and other data that potential stakeholders will study. It also addresses the responsibilities of financial advisers in assuring the quality and completeness of financial data.

Legal and Compliance Considerations

Ensuring legal and regulatory compliance is vital. This section addresses the legal implications of transition, including contract evaluations, intellectual property rights, and any outstanding legal concerns. It also gives insights on how to solve compliance problems and reduce legal risks.

Operational Optimization

Optimizing your business's processes is vital for a successful transition. This section examines ways to simplify your operations, enhance efficiency, and find areas where cost reduction and performance increase are conceivable. It also discusses the need to document important operating processes and have a well-defined organizational structure.

Customer and Employee Relations

Maintaining solid ties with consumers and staff is crucial throughout a transformation. This section digs into ways to ensure that clients continue to get the quality goods or services they expect. It also outlines communication tactics for resolving employee concerns and keeping important personnel throughout the shift.

Managing Intellectual Property

Intellectual property plays a key part in the value of your firm. This section discusses ways to safeguard and administer intellectual property rights, including trademarks, copyrights, patents, and trade secrets. It also addresses how to transfer or license these assets during a transition.

Contingency Planning

Preparing for unanticipated problems is an element of good transition planning. This section outlines contingency planning, including building backup plans and techniques to meet unanticipated challenges that may emerge throughout the transition process.

Due Diligence and Third-Party Assessments

Prospective buyers, partners, or investors typically do due diligence to determine the worth and risks connected with your organization. This section analyzes the due diligence process and describes how to prepare for third-party evaluations, answer queries, and give the appropriate paperwork and access.

The Emotional Side of Exiting

Exiting a firm is not just a financial and strategic choice but also an emotional one. This chapter is devoted to studying the often-overlooked emotional components of the departure process. Understanding and managing the emotional aspect of departing is key to a successful and happy transition.

Recognizing Emotional Complexities

Before diving into methods, it's crucial to appreciate the emotional difficulties that entrepreneurs encounter throughout the departure process. This section covers the spectrum of feelings that may develop, from elation and relief to uncertainty, fear, and even mourning. Acknowledging these feelings is the first step to properly controlling them.

Coping with Change

Exit delivers a considerable shift to an entrepreneur's life. This section explores how to deal with change, adjust to a new reality, and find purpose and satisfaction outside your company. It covers the psychological and emotional issues that might develop during a change and solutions for addressing them.

Communicating with Stakeholders

Effective communication with stakeholders, including workers, customers, and investors, is a critical component in managing the emotional side of exiting. This section digs into ways for truthful and sympathetic communication that answers problems, creates trust, and promotes healthy relationships.

Support Systems and Networks

Leveraging support systems and networks may give emotional resilience throughout a departure. This section addresses the necessity of receiving guidance, mentoring, and emotional support from trustworthy persons, such as friends, family, and peer networks. It also highlights the function of expert counselors in supporting you through emotional issues.

Defining Life Beyond Business

Exiting a firm typically generates thoughts about what comes next. This part invites you to develop a vision for life outside your company, whether it means exploring new businesses, enjoying personal hobbies, or contributing to societal concerns. It gives insights into establishing a satisfying post-exit life plan.

Managing Stress and Self-Care
Managing stress and exercising self-care are crucial parts of emotional well-being during an exit. This section highlights tools for stress management, including mindfulness, meditation, exercise, and other self-care activities that may help you negotiate the emotional journey.

The Impact on Identity and Self-Worth
Entrepreneurs frequently connect deeply with their firms, and departing may have a dramatic influence on identity and self-worth. This section examines ways to harmonize your identity outside your company and cultivate self-worth that isn't entirely related to your entrepreneurial career.

Legacy and Impact
Leaving a good legacy and having an influence outside your firm is a gratifying component of quitting. This section explores ways to ensure your leaving adds to the legacy you wish to leave and produces a lasting influence on your community or business.

- # The Serial Entrepreneur's Mindset

Serial entrepreneurs possess a distinct mentality that drives their ability to continually start, expand, exit, and repeat enterprises effectively. This chapter discusses the critical attributes and mentality features that define serial entrepreneurs as distinct and lead to their continuous success in the Entrepreneur's Loop.

Vision and Opportunity Recognition

Serial entrepreneurs possess a high sense of vision and opportunity detection. This section explains how to build the capacity to spot possible possibilities in the market, discover gaps, and envisage solutions that may lead to profitable initiatives. It underlines the significance of keeping interested and open to new ideas.

Risk Tolerance and Resilience

A willingness to take measured risks is a trademark of serial entrepreneurs. This section covers how to establish a healthy risk tolerance and resilience, realizing that setbacks and failures are part of the entrepreneurial path. It gives ways to bounce back from hurdles and learn from setbacks.

Adaptability and Continuous Learning

Serial entrepreneurs are very adaptive and always want to learn and improve. This section emphasizes the significance of adjusting to changing market circumstances, adopting new technology, and remaining current on industry trends. It also highlights the benefits of a development mindset that supports constant learning.

Resourcefulness and Creativity

Resourcefulness and ingenuity are crucial attributes for serial entrepreneurs. This section discusses ways to find innovative solutions to challenges, make the most of limited resources, and think beyond the box. It underlines the significance of innovation and creativity in the enterprise.

Networking and Relationship Building

Building a solid network is crucial for serial entrepreneurs. This section digs into the art of networking, and developing connections with mentors, advisers, partners, and other entrepreneurs. It gives insights on how to harness your network for support, advice, and opportunities.

Persistence and Determination
Serial entrepreneurs demonstrate persistent tenacity and commitment. This section explores ways to keep motivation and attention even when confronted with hurdles and disappointments. It illustrates the necessity of defining clear objectives and being devoted to attaining them.

Time Management and Prioritization
Effective time management and prioritizing are crucial for serial entrepreneurs managing many companies. This section examines time management tactics, including defining priorities, allocating chores, and making optimal use of your time. It addresses the significance of discipline in managing your time successfully.

Mentorship and Giving Back
Serial entrepreneurs generally value mentoring and giving back to the entrepreneurial community. This section highlights the advantages of both seeking and offering to mentor. It analyzes the feeling of satisfaction that comes from mentoring others in their business adventures.

Long-Term Vision and Legacy
Serial entrepreneurs see beyond individual endeavors and generally have a long-term vision and a desire

to leave a lasting impact. This part invites you to identify your long-term goal, whether it entails growing a commercial empire, contributing to humanitarian issues, or leaving a legacy that stretches beyond your lifetime.

• Learning from Past Ventures

One of the distinguishing traits of serial entrepreneurs is their ability to extract useful lessons and insights from each business, whether it's a success or a loss. This chapter discusses the skill of learning from prior initiatives and applying those experiences to influence future entrepreneurial attempts.

The Value of Reflecting on Past Ventures

Before getting into tactics, it's vital to recognize the benefit of reflecting on prior initiatives. This section explores why learning from the past is crucial in personal and professional progress. It stresses that every event, regardless of the result, carries useful lessons.

Conducting Post-Mortems

Conducting post-mortems, or organized evaluations, is a great technique to examine the strengths and faults of prior projects. This section gives a framework for doing post-mortems, including examining what went well, what went wrong, and what might have been done differently. It also highlights the significance of impartiality in self-assessment.

Identifying Patterns and Trends

Serial entrepreneurs typically notice patterns and trends that reoccur across enterprises. This section addresses how to spot recurring themes, obstacles, or opportunities that appear throughout your entrepreneurial path. Identifying these trends might guide your decision-making in future initiatives.

Building a Personal Knowledge Base

Building a personal knowledge base is vital for serial entrepreneurs. This section covers ways to capture and arrange the lessons learned from earlier efforts. It emphasizes the benefits of having a library of insights that you may resort to in future decision-making.

Mentorship and Advisors

Seeking mentoring and guidance from seasoned entrepreneurs might give you new views on your former projects. This section highlights the necessity of using mentoring and advisory ties to get insights and direction. It also explains how to pick the correct mentors and advisers.

Feedback and Continuous Improvement

Serial entrepreneurs accept feedback as a tool for continual growth. This section looks into the necessity of receiving input from team members, consumers, and stakeholders. It also addresses how to utilize feedback to develop your methods and boost your future projects.

Incorporating Lessons in New Ventures

Incorporating lessons acquired into new endeavors is a vital stage. This section discusses ways to apply your insights and make educated choices based on prior experiences. It demonstrates how a proactive attitude to learning may lead to improved success in future efforts.

Managing Risk with Informed Decisions

Serial entrepreneurs leverage their prior experiences to make educated judgments and handle risks successfully. This section covers how using lessons gained may help you analyze and minimize risks, thereby raising the odds of success in your future projects.

• Leveraging Experience in New Startups

Serial entrepreneurs possess a lot of expertise gathered from earlier companies, and they exploit this experience to boost their chances of success in future businesses. This chapter discusses techniques for successfully leveraging your experience, expertise, and insights while beginning new companies.

Harnessing the Power of Experience

Before getting into tactics, it's vital to appreciate the power of experience. This section covers the significant value that your collected expertise and lessons from earlier companies provide to your new startups. It underlines the particular advantages you have as a serial entrepreneur.

Evaluating Market Opportunities

Serial entrepreneurs are proficient at analyzing market possibilities. This section covers ways to discover new market opportunities and niches based on your expertise and insights. It addresses how to perform market research, analyze demand, and find holes in the market.

Refining Business Models

Your expertise may help you modify and change your company model to better meet market circumstances. This section goes into ways for fine-tuning your company model, pricing tactics, income sources, and value proposition depending on what you've learned from earlier endeavors.

Building a Strong Team

Serial entrepreneurs generally develop excellent teams from the beginning. This section addresses how to leverage your expertise in team building, including selecting the appropriate personnel, developing a collaborative culture, and using your network to construct a strong team for your new enterprise.

Avoiding Common Pitfalls

Leveraging experience also means avoiding typical traps. This section gives insights for spotting probable problems and traps based on your prior experiences. It addresses how to establish methods to reduce these risks and make educated judgments.

Innovation and Adaptation

Serial entrepreneurs are good at invention and adaptability. This section discusses ways to integrate innovation into your new companies, including embracing new technology, developing innovative solutions, and keeping ahead of industry trends.

Effective Resource Allocation

Your expertise may guide resource allocation for the best efficiency. This section outlines tactics for successful resource management, from budgeting to selecting investments that will promote development and success in your new firm.

Customer Acquisition and Retention

Serial entrepreneurs frequently have a strong grasp of consumer acquisition and retention. This part digs into ways to get new consumers and maintain them, building on your understanding of client habits, preferences, and successful marketing approaches.

Strategic Networking and Partnerships

Leveraging your network is a tremendous advantage. This section describes how to utilize your network to develop strategic alliances, obtain support from industry leaders, and access resources that may help your new firm grow.

• Balancing Risk and Opportunity

Successful serial entrepreneurs possess the ability to negotiate the difficult balance between taking risks and capitalizing on opportunities. This chapter discusses the tactics and mentality necessary to make educated judgments while handling the inherent hazards of entrepreneurship.

The Duality of Risk and Opportunity

Before getting into tactics, it's necessary to comprehend the duality of risk and opportunity. This section addresses the inescapable link between these two components of entrepreneurship. It highlights that possibilities typically come with underlying dangers, and handling them is the key to success.

Calculated Risk-Taking

Serial entrepreneurs are experts at taking measured risks. This section discusses ways to analyze risks, including evaluating possible outcomes, repercussions, and probability. It also stresses the significance of undertaking extensive risk assessments before making judgments.

Opportunity Identification

Identifying opportunities is a basic ability of serial entrepreneurs. This section examines ways to spot opportunities in diverse market circumstances, industries, and settings. It underlines the significance of continual scanning, market research, and being updated about developing trends.

Risk Mitigation Strategies

Effectively managing risks includes having mitigation mechanisms in place. This section goes into risk reduction measures, including diversification, contingency planning, and risk hedging. It gives insights on establishing safety nets for your enterprises.

Scenario Planning

Scenario planning is a valuable tool for managing risk and opportunity. This section covers how to utilize scenario planning to predict numerous alternative outcomes for your initiatives. It describes how this technique helps you adjust to shifting conditions.

Mentorship and Advisors

Leveraging mentoring and guidance may give fresh views on balancing risk and opportunity. This section covers the benefits of getting counsel from experienced mentors and advisers who may give insights and help you make educated choices.

Embracing Change

Embracing change is crucial for managing risks and exploiting opportunities. This part covers how to create a flexible and adaptive attitude that helps you to react to changes in the market and industry dynamics.

Resource Allocation and Opportunity Cost

Balancing risk and opportunity demands judicious resource allocation. This section digs into ways to manage resources effectively, including selecting investments that correspond with your company objectives and evaluating opportunity costs.

Tracking Key Performance Indicators (KPIs)

Effective decision-making entails monitoring KPIs. This section highlights the need to measure and monitor key performance indicators to analyze the success and effect of your operations. It also demonstrates how KPIs may influence your risk management strategy.

- # Adaptations in the Modern Business Landscape

The contemporary business world is always shifting, bringing both obstacles and possibilities for entrepreneurs. In this chapter, we cover the major adjustments that serial entrepreneurs and firms must make to flourish in today's dynamic and ever-changing world.

The Rapid Pace of Change

Before digging into particular adjustments, it's vital to appreciate the quick rate of change in the current business scene. Factors such as technical developments, market upheavals, and altering customer behavior are transforming sectors more fast than ever.

Embracing Digital Transformation

Digital transformation is at the forefront of current business operations. Serial entrepreneurs highlight the necessity of embracing technology to boost operations, reach new audiences, and maximize customer experiences. This involves the deployment of e-commerce platforms, data analytics, artificial intelligence, and more.

Agility and Flexibility

Serial entrepreneurs underline the necessity for agility and adaptability in company operations. Staying adaptive helps firms to pivot in response to changing market circumstances, unanticipated problems, and new opportunities. Flexibility in operations, supply chains, and personnel management is vital.

Customer-Centric Focus

A customer-centric strategy is a characteristic of current corporate success. Serial entrepreneurs advocate for firms to focus on understanding consumer requirements, expectations, and feedback. This emphasis on clients allows the creation of goods and services that resonate with the market.

Sustainability and Social Responsibility

The current corporate landscape increasingly prioritizes sustainability and social responsibility. Serial entrepreneurs propose that firms should incorporate ethical and ecologically concerned methods into their operations. Demonstrating a commitment to sustainability may attract environmentally conscientious customers and investment.

Remote and Hybrid Work Models

The COVID-19 epidemic boosted the adoption of remote and hybrid work styles. Serial entrepreneurs emphasize the advantages of remote work, such as accessing a global talent pool and minimizing overhead expenses. They also underline the need to successfully manage remote personnel.

Innovative Marketing and Branding

In the digital era, smart marketing and branding techniques are important. Serial entrepreneurs push firms to adopt content marketing, influencer collaborations, and social media involvement to connect with their target audiences. Building a strong web presence and a captivating brand narrative is vital.

Evolving Sales Channels

Sales channels have expanded dramatically in the current corporate world. Serial entrepreneurs propose adjusting to new sales methods, such as e-commerce, direct-to-consumer (DTC) techniques, and subscription-based services. These models provide convenience and tailored experiences to consumers.

Data-Driven Decision-Making

Data-driven decision-making is a vital adaptation. Serial entrepreneurs underline the usefulness of data analytics to guide company plans. Leveraging data may aid in spotting trends, customer behavior, and opportunities for improvement.

Cybersecurity and Privacy Concerns

As organizations become more digital, the necessity of cybersecurity and preserving consumer privacy cannot be emphasized. Serial entrepreneurs are advised to invest in effective cybersecurity measures and maintain compliance with data protection legislation.

Resilience in Uncertain Times

Building resilience is an overriding concept in current business adaptations. Serial entrepreneurs realize that uncertainty is unavoidable, and firms must prepare for unanticipated upheavals. This involves developing contingency planning, diversifying supply lines, and building a buffer against economic swings.

Inclusivity and Diversity

Inclusivity and diversity in the workplace are key adjustments. Serial entrepreneurs highlight the benefits of varied teams that bring various views and ideas to the table. Promoting inclusion and diversity creates creativity and a pleasant work atmosphere.

- ## Technology and Innovation in Serial Entrepreneurship

Technology and innovation are at the core of serial entrepreneurship. In this chapter, we look into the critical role of technology and innovation in the journeys of serial entrepreneurs, studying how they utilize these factors to generate success in their companies.

The Technological Revolution

Before getting into particular insights, it's vital to realize the technology revolution that has altered industries and entrepreneurship. Advancements in fields like artificial intelligence, cloud computing, the Internet of Things, and blockchain have opened new possibilities for innovation.

Embracing Technological Advancements

Serial entrepreneurs are noted for their ability to accept technology developments. They underline the necessity of remaining educated about upcoming technologies and trends that have the potential to disrupt or improve their industry.

Digital Transformation

Digital transformation is a prominent topic in the tales of serial entrepreneurs. They push for embracing digital technologies to improve operations, increase customer experiences, and remain competitive. This involves the use of digital technologies, e-commerce platforms, and data-driven decision-making.

Innovating in Product Development

Innovation in product creation is a fundamental driver of success. Serial entrepreneurs underline the necessity to generate distinctive and high-quality goods or services that fulfill growing market expectations. They typically utilize technology to build cutting-edge solutions.

Adapting to Market Changes

Serial entrepreneurs respond to market shifts by becoming early adopters of technical innovations. They highlight the significance of flexibility and being fast to pivot when market circumstances vary, employing technology to grasp new possibilities.

Data Analytics and Customer Insights

Data analytics is a useful tool for serial entrepreneurs. They underline the necessity of obtaining and analyzing data to acquire insights into consumer behavior, market trends, and development opportunities. Data-driven decision-making informs their tactics.

AI and Automation

Artificial intelligence and automation play a crucial part in contemporary entrepreneurship. Serial entrepreneurs utilize the potential of AI and automation to streamline operations, increase consumer relationships, and cut expenses. These technologies boost efficiency and scalability.

Blockchain and Cryptocurrencies

Blockchain technology and cryptocurrencies have opened up new options for serial entrepreneurs. They examine the uses of blockchain in domains including supply chain management, digital identity verification, and secure transactions. Cryptocurrencies are also explored in payment choices and financial strategy.

Sustainability and Green Tech

Sustainability is an area of innovation for serial entrepreneurs. They invest in green technology and eco-friendly solutions to line with rising environmental concerns. This involves producing renewable energy alternatives, eco-conscious goods, and sustainable corporate practices.

Cybersecurity and Data Privacy

With the rising digitalization of business, cybersecurity, and data privacy are crucial. Serial entrepreneurs underline the significance of investing in effective cybersecurity solutions to secure their companies and client data.

Leveraging Emerging Trends

Serial entrepreneurs harness new developments, such as the Internet of Things (IoT), augmented reality, and virtual reality, to create unique and market-disrupting goods and experiences. Staying at the forefront of trends may distinguish their efforts.

Building Tech-Driven Teams

Building teams with tech-savvy individuals is vital. Serial entrepreneurs highlight the significance of developing teams that can manage and utilize technology successfully, from engineers and data scientists to digital marketing professionals.

Open Innovation and Collaboration

Open innovation entails engaging with external partners, startups, and research institutes to stimulate creativity and bring new ideas to your enterprises. Serial entrepreneurs are open to cooperation as a strategy to stimulate innovation.

• Global Perspectives on Entrepreneurship

Entrepreneurship is a dynamic and worldwide phenomenon, driven by numerous cultural, economic, and geopolitical forces. In this chapter, we study the global views on entrepreneurship, analyzing how entrepreneurship varies and flourishes throughout different parts of the globe.

The Universality of Entrepreneurship

Before digging into regional viewpoints, it's vital to acknowledge the universality of entrepreneurship. Entrepreneurship is a common thread that binds individuals throughout the globe, expressing the human yearning for innovation, opportunity, and economic empowerment.

North America: Innovation and Tech Hubs

North America is recognized for its innovation and technological centers, with Silicon Valley in California acting as a worldwide emblem. Serial entrepreneurs from this area highlight the significance of technical innovation, venture capital networks, and a culture that supports risk-taking.

Europe: Diversity and Collaboration

Europe features a broad entrepreneurial scene, with startups and firms spanning many sectors. Serial entrepreneurs here underline the benefits of teamwork, access to a vast talent pool, and backing from the European Union for cross-border efforts.

Asia: Rapid Growth and Innovation

Asia is characterized by fast economic expansion and a strong concentration on innovation. Serial entrepreneurs from nations like China, India, and Singapore stress the necessity for agility, a thorough grasp of local markets, and relationships with Asian tech giants.

Africa: Social Entrepreneurship and Impact

Africa has experienced a boom in social entrepreneurship, with firms committed to tackling critical societal concerns. Serial entrepreneurs on the continent stress the significance of impact-driven business models, sustainable development, and harnessing mobile technologies to reach underprivileged populations.

Latin America: Entrepreneurial Spirit and Resilience

Latin America is noted for its entrepreneurial drive and perseverance in the face of economic hardships. Serial entrepreneurs from this area underline the need for tenacity, the ability to negotiate bureaucratic impediments, and the use of local ecosystems for development.

Middle East: Investment and Technology Adoption

The Middle East has experienced tremendous investment in entrepreneurship, notably in nations like the United Arab Emirates and Israel. Serial entrepreneurs underline the necessity of responding to technology advancements and tapping into investment possibilities in the area.

Oceania: Environmental Sustainability and Innovation

Oceania, notably Australia and New Zealand, is focused on environmental sustainability and creative solutions. Serial entrepreneurs stress the necessity of eco-conscious enterprises, access to research institutes, and worldwide alliances for impact.

Emerging Markets: Navigating Challenges

Entrepreneurship in developing economies has distinct obstacles. Serial entrepreneurs from these locations emphasize adaptation, local collaborations, and resilience in the face of economic swings and regulatory changes.

The Role of Globalization

Globalization has linked entrepreneurs and marketplaces globally. Serial entrepreneurs advocate for utilizing the advantages of globalization, including cross-border cooperation, access to global talent, and worldwide growth.

Cultural Awareness and Sensitivity

Entrepreneurs functioning in global situations highlight the significance of cultural understanding and sensitivity. Understanding local cultures, communication styles, and market intricacies is vital for creating trust and effective commercial connections.

Solving Global Challenges

Serial entrepreneurs throughout the world have a shared purpose of tackling global concerns. They stress the benefits of commercial enterprises that target challenges like climate change, healthcare access, education, and poverty on a global scale.

• Summary Of The Entrepreneur's Loop

The Entrepreneur's Loop is a continual cycle of entrepreneurship that serial entrepreneurs master over time. It comprises of four main stages: Start, Scale, Exit, and Repeat. In this cycle, entrepreneurs consistently shift from one stage to the next, employing their expertise and insights to attain success. Let's break down each stage:

1. **Start**: This is the commencement of a new company enterprise. Entrepreneurs seek possibilities, create unique concepts, and establish their enterprises. They negotiate the obstacles of market research, company strategy, and collecting first capital.

2. **Scale**: Once a firm is established, entrepreneurs work on scaling its operations. They desire quick expansion, expand into new areas, and typically confront issues relating to managing resources, establishing effective teams, and executing growth plans.

3. **Exit**: Exiting a venture may take different forms, such as selling the firm, merging with another company, or going public via an IPO. Serial entrepreneurs

understand when it's the proper moment to depart a firm and execute the exit plan efficiently.

4. **Repeat**: After departing one endeavor, serial entrepreneurs typically return to the "Start" phase with a new idea or business plan. They employ the information and experience obtained from earlier initiatives to boost their chances of success in the next entrepreneurial project.

Key Principles of the Entrepreneur's Loop:

- **Resilience**: Serial entrepreneurs build resilience, rebounding back from failures and setbacks.

- **Adaptability**: They stay adaptive, reacting to changing market circumstances and fresh possibilities.

- **Innovation**: Innovation is a continuing topic, driving the creation of distinctive goods and services.

- **Risk Management**: Serial entrepreneurs thrive at calibrated risk-taking, supported by extensive risk analysis and mitigation methods.

- **Consumer-Centricity**: They emphasize understanding consumer requirements and delivering solutions that connect with their target audience.

- **Mentorship and Collaboration**: Seeking assistance from experienced mentors and cooperating with others are standard activities.
- **Technology and Innovation**: Leveraging technology and embracing innovation is crucial to remaining competitive.
- **worldwide Perspectives**: Entrepreneurs comprehend the different problems and possibilities of entrepreneurship on a worldwide scale.

Ultimately, the Entrepreneur's Loop is a path distinguished by a dedication to continual learning, a growth mentality, and a love for developing, expanding, exiting, and repeating companies. By mastering this cycle, serial entrepreneurs attain continuous success in the dynamic world of entrepreneurship.

- # The Endless Journey of Entrepreneurship

The road of entrepreneurship is sometimes characterized as eternal, with no ultimate goal in sight. In this chapter, we examine the concept that entrepreneurship is a continuing and dynamic activity, exploring the attitude, obstacles, and benefits that come with embracing this everlasting journey.

Embracing the Continual Evolution

One of the core concepts of entrepreneurship is knowing that it's an ever-evolving adventure. Serial entrepreneurs recognize that the business environment is in perpetual upheaval, driven by technical developments, shifting customer tastes, and global economic shifts. This insight is the cornerstone of their success.

The Mindset of Lifelong Learning

Serial entrepreneurs are lifelong learners. They approach each undertaking with curiosity and a willingness to gain new information and abilities. They know that the route to mastery is paved with continual self-improvement and adaptability to new difficulties.

Resilience Amidst Uncertainty

The everlasting path of business is fraught with uncertainty and disappointments. Serial entrepreneurs are typified by their resilience, the ability to bounce back from setbacks, adapt to unanticipated situations, and keep the urge to move forward.

The Role of Mentorship

Mentorship is a guiding light throughout the business path. Serial entrepreneurs generally credit their mentors with offering useful ideas, counsel, and a larger perspective. Mentorship is a two-way street, as experienced entrepreneurs frequently become mentors themselves, passing on the knowledge they've learned.

Chasing the Next Idea

Entrepreneurs are generally motivated by the chase of the next great idea. Serial entrepreneurs can't resist the appeal of uncovering new possibilities and bringing fresh ideas to life. This unceasing thirst for invention motivates their everlasting adventure.

Balancing Risk and Reward

Serial entrepreneurs recognize that business entails a fine balance of risk and profit. They're good at analyzing the possible hazards of their initiatives while keeping an eye on the potential benefits. This rigorous review is important to their decision-making process.

Global Engagement and Impact

The contemporary entrepreneur's path recognizes no boundaries. Serial entrepreneurs have a global perspective and exploit the interconnected globe to build their companies and make a big difference. The chance to reach a global audience is an exciting feature of the infinite journey.

Sustaining Motivation and Passion

Sustaining enthusiasm and passion over the long term is no minor achievement. Serial entrepreneurs take their energy from the exhilaration of founding, growing, and reinventing enterprises. They typically find satisfaction in the trip itself, not simply the goal.

The Legacy of Giving Back

Many serial entrepreneurs aim to leave a lasting legacy by giving back to their communities and the globe. They support charity organizations, advise budding entrepreneurs, and engage in humanitarian efforts, further enhancing the unending trip.

Reflecting on Success and Failures

Serial entrepreneurs periodically stop to reflect on their achievements and disappointments. They undertake post-mortems of earlier projects, identifying lessons learned, and applying these insights to future efforts. This reflecting process adds to their development and adaptation.

- # Encouragement for Aspiring Serial Entrepreneurs

The road of serial entrepreneurship is loaded with obstacles, uncertainty, and thrilling chances. For individuals seeking to become serial entrepreneurs or who have begun on this route, the road ahead may appear overwhelming. In this chapter, we give encouragement and important guidance to inspire and empower you on your path.

Embrace the Spirit of Innovation

The heart of serial entrepreneurship pulses with invention. Embrace your inherent curiosity and drive to explore unexplored places. Be brave to disrupt the existing quo and bring new, revolutionary ideas to life.

Start with What You're Passionate About

Your business path should begin with a true passion. Identify what actually fascinates you, since it's your excitement that will sustain you through the inevitable hurdles. When you enjoy what you do, it doesn't seem like work.

Learn from Every Experience

Every initiative, whether successful or not, is a chance for development and learning. Serial entrepreneurs consider setbacks as stepping stones toward success. Take the lessons from each event and apply them to future initiatives.

Surround Yourself with a Strong Support System

Entrepreneurship may be a lonely route, but it doesn't have to be. Build a robust support structure that includes mentors, advisers, and like-minded folks who share your goal. Their instruction and support may make all the difference.

Adapt and Stay Agile

The corporate landscape is in perpetual motion. Serial entrepreneurs flourish by keeping nimble, responding to market changes, and embracing new possibilities. Be prepared to pivot as required and harness your resilience in times of uncertainty.

Mentorship and Lifelong Learning

Mentorship is a crucial asset in your business path. Seek experienced mentors who can give useful insights and help. Additionally, never stop learning. The most successful serial entrepreneurs are lifetime students, always improving their expertise.

Persevere Through Challenges

The entrepreneurial road is not without its hurdles. There will be periods of doubt, disappointment, and uncertainty. Perseverance is your biggest friend. Hold onto your vision, keep focused, and push through the hardest circumstances.

Cultivate a Global Perspective

The globe is more linked than ever before. Consider the worldwide scene in your entrepreneurial activities. Embrace chances for worldwide growth, partnerships, and the effect you can have on a global scale.

Passion for Impact

Consider the greater influence of your initiatives. Many serial entrepreneurs feel tremendous joy in developing enterprises that contribute positively to society, whether via sustainability, social responsibility, or charity. Be motivated by the desire to make a difference.

Dream Big and Start Small

Dreams and objectives might be lofty, but every journey begins with a single step. Don't be discouraged by the vastness of your vision. Begin with tiny, attainable actions, and gradually work your way toward your final objective.

Celebrate Your Wins

It's easy to get caught up in the constant chase of achievement.

Remember to appreciate your wins, no matter how minor. Acknowledge your triumphs and reward yourself for your hard work.

It's Okay to Fail

Failure is not a setback; it's a stepping stone. Serial entrepreneurs have suffered their share of setbacks, and it's part of the path. Each time you fail, you're one step closer to success.

Your Journey is Unique

Remember that your business path is uniquely yours. Don't compare yourself to others. Your route will have its twists and turns, and that's what makes it distinctive.

www.ingramcontent.com/pod-product-compliance
Lightning Source LLC
Chambersburg PA
CBHW062245290526
45794CB00006B/2415